TABLE OF CONTENTS

CONCLUSION

INTRODUCTION

Every person appreciates excellent food, specifically around the Christmas and also Hanukkah vacations. Nonetheless, if you are a diabetic or have a diabetic member of the family you probably assume that great food and a diabetic person diet plan is an oxymoron. Not real as well as I will verify it. My name is Richard Terry as well as I am a Type 2 diabetic person. I'm the author of Dick's Holiday Diabetes Cookbook. My favorite leisure activity is cooking and also having friends over for supper. I also delight in having a great glass of a glass of wine with my meals. Exactly how's that for an additional dispute of interest.

When I discovered that I was a Type 2 diabetic person I truly felt perplexed since I like good food. Rather than approve the idea of surviving on bland, unsavory food I decided to locate recipes that were wonderful as well as satisfied the diabetes mellitus dish intending needs. I establish out to find out just how to come to be a good, healthy and balanced, diabetic person cook as well as yet provide delicious dishes for my household.

Over the previous couple of years I have actually evaluated and also collected a ton of dishes from the net, other diabetic recipe books, diabetic person dieticians and several of my pals. I have explore and removed many. What is left is a collection of diabetic issues recipes that I recommend. They are very easy to follow as well as pleasing to almost any person's taste buds, diabetic person or otherwise.

Furthermore, I gathered some terrific holiday diabetic issues recipes. Due to the fact that the holiday period is also the festive food season, that truly pleased me. I am pleased to serve for your holiday food preparation and also consuming enjoyment Dick's Holiday Diabetes Cookbook, a collection of vacation food recipes that you, your family as well as your friends will definitely delight in throughout the holiday season.

When you check out this holiday recipe collection you will see that a white wine tip is made with each main course. I think that a glass of a glass of wine is the perfect enhance to any meal.While you might have heard or else, the American Diabetes Association (ADA) released a report that ended that a diabetic should utilize caution when taking in alcohol as well as to eat it with food. I was pleased to find out that I can still have a glass of white wine with my meals which is exactly why I have provided a suggested a glass of wine with each entrée in this publication.

The complete ADA Diabetes as well as Alcohol record is reprinted in the referral area of guide. I have actually also included various other tables, graphes as well as details that you may discover useful as you prepare your food selections

Each dish in the book includes my remarks about the recipe. These **Comments** are based upon my experience with the recipe as well as ideas that might be of passion to you in deciding which dish to prepare. I have likewise provided the nutritional info as well as nutritional exchanges. Guide includes entrées, appetisers, as well as desserts. I have actually also consisted of a section of Hanukkah entrées and Latkes. The entrée area has tasty tenderloin, beef rib roast, turkey, pork, as well as fish diabetic person recipes. There are desserts that fit the Christmas season. You will certainly vow they are not diabetic issues recipes.

My recipes do not need a lot of time to make and also practically no special cooking area equipment. They are very easy to adhere to make sure that also the inexperienced home chef can create a meal that will certainly be mouthwatering. Do not hesitate to experiment, include or delete seasonings and also other **Ingredients**. That's what makes food preparation enjoyable. The very best means to utilize Dick's Holiday Diabetes Cookbook is to utilize your duplicate to choose a recipe that sounds right for tonight and start cooking - it's that easy! You will certainly enjoy the experience and virtually neglect you are a diabetic.

APPETIZERS

Cranberry Cream Cheese Spread
Yield: 48 treats
Preparation time: 15 Minutes
Remarks: Quick as well as easy however tasty
Ingredients
1 (8oz) plan of fat totally free cream cheese, softened a little
1 mug cranberry chutney, fruit juice sweetened (or your favored taste chutney).
Preparation.
1. In center of serveing platter, mound lotion cheese into round with top flattened a little.
2. Pour chutney in addition to lotion cheese.
3. Serve with water biscuits.
Nutritional Information (per serving).
Calories: 13; Protein: 1 g; Sodium: 28 mg; Cholesterol: 1 mg;
Carbohydrates: 2 g; Exchanges: 1 complimentary food exchange.

Mushroom and also Bacon Petite Quiche.
Yield: 3 1/2 dozen, serveing dimension 1 petite quiche **Preparation time**: 20 mins Cook time: 40 minutes.
Remarks: Tender, mouthwatering and also tacky custards in half-cracked pastry shells make classy finger food-- as well as can be made ahead and reheated. Delicious for a Christmas breakfast or for night appetisers.
Ingredients.
8 slices bacon.
1/4 extra pound fresh mushrooms, cleaned and also cut 1 tablespoon butter.
1/3 mug environment-friendly onion, sliced.
1 2/3 cups Swiss cheese, shredded.
Pastry for double-crust pie, (homemade or acquired) 5 eggs.
1 2/3 cups sour lotion.
Prep work as well as Cooking.
1. Warm stove to 375 degrees F.

2. On a lightly floured board, turn out the bread dough 1/ 16-inch thick.

3. Making use of a 3-inch cutter, eliminated 42 circles; re-roll scraps as needed.

4. Fit circles into bottoms and also somewhat up sides of lightly greased 2-1/2- inch muffin pans.

5. Fry bacon slices until crisp, drainpipe; cut or crumble.

6. Cut mushrooms, sauté in butter until limp and fluid evaporates.

7. Incorporate bacon, mushrooms, environment-friendly onion and cheese. Split filling equally amongst muffin mugs.

8. In huge dish, defeated together eggs, add sour cream as well as mix until smooth. Spoon about 1 tbsp right into each muffin mug.

9. Bake until blown and also brown, 20-25 minutes. Trendy in frying pans 5 mins; lift out.

10. Serve warm or let cool on wire racks. If made ahead, cover cooled down quiches closed, as well as cool overnight.

11. Reheat, exposed, in a 350 levels F. stove for concerning 10 mins.

Nutritional Information (per serving).

Calories: 95; Protein: 3 g; Fat: 7 g; Sodium: 87 mg; Cholesterol: 35 mg; Dietary Fiber: 0 g; Carbohydrates: 4 g.

Stuffed Onions with Spinach Feta.

Yield: 4 servings (1 Serving = 1/2 Stuffed Onion) Prep as well as Cook time: 1 hour.

Remarks: Easy to do and also special appetiser for any vacation or other dinner events.

Ingredients.

2 huge pleasant or Spanish onions (about 1-1/2 pounds total, peeled) 2 tsps olive oil.

1 clove garlic.

One 10-ounce package icy chopped spinach, defrosted as well as squeezed dry 1 tsp fresh lemon juice.

1/4 tsp fresh ground pepper 1/4 mug bread crumbs.

1/4 mug (1 ounce) fell apart feta cheese.

Prep work as well as Cooking.

1. Location the onions in a big pan and also cover with water.

2. Serve a boil as well as cook till the onions are partially tender, concerning 10 to 15 mins. Drain as well as cool; reduce the onions in fifty percent crosswise.

3. Scoop out the facility of each onion half, leaving a 1/2-inch covering. Book the centers. If essential, reduced a tiny item from completion of each onion covering so the shells will stand upright.

4. Prepare a superficial baking meal huge enough to hold the onion halves in one layer with non-stick frying pan spray. Place the onions in the prepared dish, hollowed sides up.

5. Preheat the oven to 350 degrees F.

6. Chop the reserved centers of the onions. Sauté in oil with the garlic in a medium pan until tender, about 5 minutes.

7. Mix in the spinach, lemon juice, and pepper; cook until the liquid evaporates. Eliminate from the warm; stir in the bread crumbs and also cheese.

8. Fill up the onion coverings with the spinach combination. Cover with foil as well as bake concerning 25 mins. Serve warm.

Nutritional Information (per serveing).

Calories: 141; Protein: 5 g; Fat: 4 g; Sodium: 187 mg; Cholesterol: 6 mg;

Carbohydrates: 22 g; Dietary Exchanges:: 1 Starch, 1 Vegetable, 1 Fat.

Appetizer Meatballs.

Yield: 7 lots meatballs. Serving dimension: 7 meatballs **Preparation time**:15 minutes Cook time: 30 minutes.

Comments: These meatballs are practical to carry hand, in the fridge freezer. Serve for snacks with dipping sauces. They're terrific for making grinder sandwiches, as well. Serveed with a dip is a wonderful discussion.

Ingredients.

2 extra pounds lean ground pork 1 cup ice water.

1/4 mug soy sauce.

1/4 tsp newly ground black pepper.

Preparation and Cooking

1. Warmth oven to 375 degrees F.

2. With hands or wood spoon mix pork, water, soy sauce as well as pepper thoroughly in huge bowl.

3. Shape right into 3/4-inch rounds (combination will be fairly soft and balls will certainly not be excellent).

4. Organize very closely together in solitary layer on ungreased shallow baking frying pan, like a jelly-roll frying pan.

5. Bake for 20-30 minutes.

6. Remove from pan, as well as serve promptly with a dipping sauce, like your favored salad dressings or select from the recommendations listed below.

7. Use toothpicks to skewer meatballs to dip. Or eliminate from frying pan, freeze, cover and also cool or refrigerate. Serve cool or reheated.

Nutritional Information (per serveing).

Calories: 200; Protein: 13 g; Fat: 16 g; Sodium: 390 mg; Cholesterol: 55 mg; Carbohydrates: 1 g.

Ginger-Orange Dip.

Yield: about 20 servings (serving size: 1 tsp) **Preparation time**: 10 mins.
Comments: Great dip with appetiser meatballs, provides a burst of citrus.
Another usage is to sprinkle it on a sliced up roast beef sandwich for an
adjustment to this favored lunch.

Ingredients.

3 ounces thawed orange juice concentrate 3 tablespoons olive oil.
1 tbsp grated fresh ginger 1 garlic clove, smashed Preparation.
In medium bowl mix with each other orange juice concentrate, olive oil,
ginger and garlic. Mix well.

Nutritional Information (per serveing).

Calories: 15; Protein: 0 g; Fat: 1 g; Sodium: 0 mg; Cholesterol: 0 mg;
Carbohydrates: 1 g.

Cranberry-Barbecue Dip.

Yield: regarding 20 - 1 teaspoon servings.

Preparation time: 10 minutes Cook time: 2 minutes.

Comments: Another fantastic dip for Appetizer Meatballs. Additionally is an excellent last polish for grilled pork, turkey or poultry.

Ingredients.

1/2 cup cranberry sauce 1/2 mug barbeque sauce **Preparation and Cooking**

1. In tool dish, mix with each other cranberry sauce and also barbeque sauce; cover loosely as well as heat in microwave on 50% power for 2 minutes.

Nutritional Information (per serving).

Calories: 5; Protein: 0 g; Sodium: 20 mg; Cholesterol: 0 mg; Carbohydrates: 1 g.

Toasted Onion Meatball Dip

Yield: About 20 1 teaspoon servings Preparation time: regarding 15 mins.

Comments: Flavorful dip for your appetizer meatballs or with various other crudités. Functions well as a sandwich spread.

Ingredients.

1/2 cup plain yogurt.

1/2 cup low-fat sour cream.

2 tablespoons dried out onion soup mix, or regarding 1/2 of 1-ounce bundle driedonion soup mix.

1 tablespoon Dijon-style mustard.

Preparation.

1. In medium dish stir together yogurt, sour lotion, onion soup mix, Dijon-style mustard. Mix well.

Nutritional Information (per serveing).

Calories: 15; Protein: 1 g; Sodium: 100.

Basil Yogurt Dip.

Yield: About 1 mug.

Preparation time: 1 hr as well as 10 minutes (consists of cool time in refrigerator) **Comments**: Easy to do and is a great dip with a variety of raw veggies. **Ingredients**.

3/4 cup simple low-fat yogurt.

1/4 mug cholesterol-free reduced-calorie mayonnaise or salad clothing 1/4 tsp salt.

1/2 cup watercress leaves 1/2 mug fresh parsley leaves 1/4 mug fresh basil leaves.

1 environment-friendly onion (with top), cut into 1-inch pieces.

Prep work.

1. Place yogurt, mayo and also salt in blender or food processor or food processor. Include continuing to be **Ingredients**. Cover and also mix or process regarding 30 seconds, stopping blender occasionally to scratch sides, till carefully sliced.

2. Cover and refrigerate concerning 1 hour or till slightly thickened as well as chilled.

Nutritional Information (per serving).

Calories: 20; Protein: 1 g; Fat: 1 g; Sodium: 75 mg; Cholesterol: 0 mg; Carbohydrates: 1 g; Dietary Exchanges: Free.

Cheesy Zucchini Bites.

Yield: 35 servings.

Preparation time: 10 minutes Cook time: 7 minutes.

Comments: Easy to make and also taste so excellent you need to be careful not to eat excessive as well as ruin your supper.

Ingredients.

5 tool zucchini (concerning 6 inches long) 4 ounces blue cheese, crumbled.

3 tbsps grated Parmesan cheese 1 teaspoon dried out basil.

1/8 teaspoon pepper.

1 pint cherry tomatoes, very finely cut.

Preparation and Cooking

1. Incorporate the Parmesan basil, pepper, and also cheese; mi x fifty

percent with blue cheese. Sprinkle on each zucchini, then sprinkle with the remaining Parmesan combination.

2. Bake at 400 ° F up until cheese is thawed, 5-7 mins. Serve cozy.

Nutritional details (per serving).

Calories: 19; Saturated Fat: 1 g; Cholesterol: 3mg; Sodium: 58mg: Carbohydrates: 1g; Protein: 1g.

DINNER ENTREES.

Vacation Rib Roast with Dijon-Sour Cream Sauce.

Yield: 8 servings, 4 ounces cooked beef and 1 1/2 tablespoons sauce.

Preparation time: 20 minutes, plus 24 hr marinate.

Prepare time: 2 1/4 hours, plus 15 mins stand time.

Remarks: No Christmas is total without serving a rib roast. It is a great tradition that my household always complies with. This specific recipe with the Dijon-sour sauce is superior.

Ingredients.

4 - extra pound beef rib roast, cut of fat.

3/4 cup completely dry red wine or lower-sodium beef brew 1/4 cup lemon juice.

2 teaspoons dried out rosemary, crushed 2 teaspoons dried marjoram, crushed 1/4 tsp garlic salt.

1 dish Dijon-Sour Cream Sauce (below).

Preparation and Cooking

1. Place meat in a huge re-sealable plastic bag set in a superficial dish. For sauce: In a small dish combine white wine, lemon juice, rosemary, marjoram, and garlic salt. Put over meat. Seal bag; rely on layer meat. Season in the refrigerator for at the very least 6 hrs or approximately 24 hours, turning bag periodically. Drain meat, discarding marinade.

2. Preheat oven to 350 levels F.

3. Area roast, fat side up, in an ungreased 13x9x2-inch baking pan or 3-quart cooking meal.

4. Insert an ovenproof meat thermostat into the facility of the roast. The thermostat needs to not touch the bone.

5. Roast, uncovered, up until preferred doneness. Enable 1-3/4 to 2-1/4 hours for tool unusual (135 degrees F) or 2-1/4 to 2-3/4 hrs for medium (150 levels F). Cover with foil; allow stand 15 mins. The temperature level of the meat after standing must be 145 degrees F for medium uncommon or 160 levels F for tool.

6. Carve roast and serve with Dijon-Sour Cream Sauce. Makes 8 (4 ounces

cooked beef as well as 1-1/2 tablespoons sauce each) servings.

Dijon-Sour Cream Sauce **Ingredients**.

1 8-ounce carton light sour cream 2 tablespoons Dijon-style mustard.

1/2 teaspoon sodium-free lemon-pepper spices Preparation.

1. In a small bowl mix together sour cream, mustard, as well as lemon-pepper spices. Cover as well as cool till serving time.

Suggested wine: A nice Cabernet Sauvignon.

Nutrition Facts (per serving).

Fat,: 8g; Chol.: 12 mg; Sat. fat: 6g; Monosaturated fat: 5g; Cal.: 258 kcal; Protein: 30g; Carbs.: 2g; Sodium: 263 mg; Iron: 3 mg; Calcium: 50 mg; Potassium: 517 (mg); Trans fat: 0g; Sugar: 0 g; Fiber: 0 g; Polyunsaturated fat: 0 g; Diabetic Exchanges; Carb Choice (d.e): 0, Fat (d.e): 1.5, Lean Meat (d.e): 4.

Crown Roast of Pork with Walnut-Rhubarb Stuffing.

Serves 16.

Preparation time: 45 minutesCook time: 2-1/2 hours.

Comments: This makes a lovely presentation to slice at your vacation table. I frequently place part of the dressing in the facility of the roast. Serve with a green vegetable and side salad.

Ingredients.

8-9 extra pound crown roast of pork salt, to taste.

pepper, to taste.

1 extra pound ground pork, cooked and also crumbled 5 mugs completely dry bread cubes.

1 14 1/2- oz can hen brew 1/2 mug onion, cut.

1/2 cup celery, cut.

1cup walnut fifty percents, toasted 1 tsp salt.

1/4 tsp cinnamon 1/4 tsp allspice.

1/8 teaspoon ground black pepper.

2cups rhubarb, diced (fresh or icy, thawed) 1/2 cup sugar.

Directions.

1. Heat stove to 350 levels F. Generously period pork with salt and pepper; area in shallow toasting frying pan; roast for about 2 1/2 hours (about 20 mins per pound), till internal temperature level on a thermometer reads 145 levels F. Remove roast from stove; allow rest regarding 10 mins prior to cutting to serve with stuffing.

2. At the same time, in huge dish completely combine ground pork, bread cubes, broth, onion, celery, walnuts and also seasonings; mix well. In medium saucepan, combine rhubarb as well as sugar; give a boil. Put over stuffing blend; mix gently. Spoon right into buttered 2-quart covered dish. Cover, bake at 350 degrees F. for 1 1/2 hrs.

A glass of wine pointer: A great Beaujolais or Pinot Noir.

Nutritional Information Per Serving.

Calories: 590; Protein: 60 g; Fat: 22 g; Sodium: 670 mg; Cholesterol: 145 mg; Saturated Fat: 7 g; Carbohydrates: 33 g.

Peanuts and also Applesauce-Stuffed Pork Tenderloin.

Yield: 6 servings.

Preparation time: 15 mins Cook time: 25 mins.

Remarks: Makes a nice presentation as well as preference scrumptious, perfect dish throughout the holiday season.

Ingredients.

2 pork tenderloins, 1 pound each 1/4 cup apple juice, OR vermouth 2/3 cup beefy applesauce.

1/4 cup completely dry roasted peanuts, carefully sliced 1/4 teaspoon fennel seed, finely crushed 1/4 teaspoon salt.

Preparation and Cooking

1. Warmth oven to 425 levels F.

2. Using a sharp knife, form a "pocket" in each tenderloin by cutting a lengthwise slit down facility of each almost to, however not through, bottom of each tenderloin. Area tenderloins in shallow toasting frying pan.

3. In small dish stir with each other apple juice, applesauce, peanuts, salt, pepper and also fennel.

4. Spoon blend right into pocket of each tenderloin. Secure packed pockets with toothpicks.

5. Roast for 20 minutes till inner temperature level on a thermometer checks out 160 levels F and let stand 5 mins prior to slicing to serve.

Suggested wine: Either a great white, Pinot Grigio or red Pinot Noir.

Nutritional Information (per serveing).

Calories: 200; Protein: 32 g; Fat: 5 g; Sodium: 170 mg; Cholesterol: 100 mg; Dietary Fiber: 0 g; Carbohydrates: 4 g.

Adobo-Crusted Lamb Loin Chops.

Yield: 4 servings.

Preparation time: 25 minutes Cook time: 17 minutes.

Comments: I had never tried Adobo crust before this dish. It is great as well as serves an actual vacation spirit to this entrée. Keep in mind do not over chef the lamb.

Ingredients.

1tablespoon fennel seed 1 tbsp cumin seed.

2teaspoons coriander seed 1/2 tsp dried rosemary 2 tsps fractured pepper 1/2 tsp kosher salt.

2 teaspoons minced garlic 2 teaspoons dried out oregano 1/2 teaspoon dried out thyme 2 teaspoons lime zest.

8 lamb loin chops, 1-inch thick 4 tablespoons olive oil.

Preparation and Cooking

1. In a completely dry frying pan, salute fennel, cumin, coriander, rosemary and also pepper for a couple of mins until fragrant; let cool and grind coarsely in a flavor mill or mixer.

2. Stir in salt, garlic, oregano, thyme and lime passion.

3. Massage both sides of each lamb chop with about a tbsp of the spice mixture; cover as well as allow mean at least 1 hour.

4. Preheat oven to 400F.

5. Warmth two oven-proof large frying pans over medium-high heat; include 2 tbsps of olive oil per frying pan as well as bring simply to the smoking point.

6. Place 4 lamb chops in each warm pan and also burn for 5 mins; transform lamb to sear the 2nd side for an added 2 mins.

7. Position the pans into the stove and continue to prepare the chops for 5 to 10 minutes or till lamb is cooked to your liking.

Suggested a glass of wine: A wonderful Pinot Noir.

Nutritional Information (per serveing).

Calories: 316; Protein: 25 g; Fat: 22 g; Sodium: 307 mg; Cholesterol: 80 mg; Dietary Fiber: 2 g; Carbohydrates: 4 g.

Cornbread and Apple -Stuffed Pork Loin with Apple Gravy

Yield: 8 serving
Preparation time: 45 minutes
Cook time: 1 hr
Remarks: While it looks difficult, it is really fairly easy to prepare and also prepare. When you are done you will certainly have a cheery Christmas creation that is remarkably tasty.

Ingredients
1 boneless pork loin, (4 pounds) kosher salt
freshly ground black pepper 1 tsp dried sage
3 tool apples, peeled off, cut in half, cored and also cut right into 1/2-inch slices 1/4 mug Calvados, OR apple brandy
1-1/4 mug homemade chicken supply, OR canned low-sodium poultry broth
1 cup apple juice, OR cider 1/4 mug whipping cream
Cornbread as well as Apple Stuffing **Ingredients**: 1-1/2 tbsps butter
1/2 cup smoked pork, finely chopped, OR diced smoked sausage 1/2 mug onion, carefully cut
1/4 mug celery, carefully sliced kosher salt
fresh ground black pepper
3/4 mug apples, peeled and diced 1/4-inch 1/2 tsp dried sage
1-1/2 mugs homemade cornbread, collapsed as well as dried out OR dried cornbread padding mix
1/4 mug apple juice
Preparation as well as Cooking
1. For stuffing, warm butter in a heavy tool frying pan over medium-low warm; include pork or sausage and chef 3 mins. Include onion, celery and a pinch each of salt as well as pepper; cover and chef, stirring occasionally, until the veggies are rather soft, concerning 10 minutes.
2. Stir in diced apple and cook 1 minute. Transfer apple mix to a big dish. Sprinkle with sage as well as stir in cornbread crumbs, apple juice and also egg. The mix must be not wet however moist. If the mix seems dry, add a lot more apple juice. Taste for spices and set aside.
3. Preheat stove to 450 levels F. To double butterfly the pork loin, lay the

meat, fat-side down, on a work surface area as well as make a horizontal lengthwise cut two-thirds of the method right into the deepness of the loin and also regarding 1 inch from the long side nearest you, taking care not to cut completely via.

4. Flip the loin over to ensure that the cut you just made is opposite you. Make another lengthwise cut, once more 1 inch from the side. Open up the two cuts so you have a huge rectangular shape of meat whose size is roughly 3 times the density of the meat.

5. Place fat-side down and also cover with a sheet of plastic wrap. Utilizing the flat side of a cleaver or a meat pounder, gently flatten the meat to an also density.

6. Remove cling wrap as well as spread apple stuffing equally over the meat, leaving a charitable 3/4-- inch border. Roll up meat jelly-roll style so that padding remains in a spiral pattern. Tie rolled roast at 2-inch periods with butcher's twine.

7. Combine 2 teaspoons salt, 1 tsp pepper, and remaining sage and sprinkle over roast.

8. Lay the chopped apples on the bottom of a toasting frying pan just a bit larger than the roast as well as established the roast, fat-side up, on the apples.

9. Put roast in the stove and chef for 15 minutes, transform the oven down to 325 levels as well as roast for 45 mins. Inspect the interior temperature level of the roast with an instant-read thermometer: The roast is done when it reaches 145 degrees. If it is not prepared, continue to roast, checking the temperature level every 10 mins.

10. When the roast is done, move it to a cutting board, tent loosely with foil, as well as allow remainder for at the very least 10 mins while you make the sauce.

11. With a slotted spoon, move the apples in the toasting pan to a bowl and keep warm. Pour off any fat from the roasting pan, leaving the meat juices under. Place frying pan over medium-high heat, add Calvados as well as deglaze pan enabling the alcohol to burn off, about 15 secs.

12. Transfer to a tiny saucepan and add stock, apple juice as well as lotion. Boost warmth to high as well as bring fluid to a boil. Simmer, mixing, till

decreased by fifty percent. Preference for salt and pepper. Keep the sauce warm while you sculpt the pork roast.

13. Get rid of twine from the roast as well as suffice into 1/2-inch thick pieces. (If you reduced the slices also thin, they will fall apart.) Arrange the pork on an serveing plate. Spoon the sliced apples around the meat and also put the sauce over all.

Suggested Wine: Gewürztraminer, a semi-sweet gewurztraminer with a jasmine, orange blossom nose and also apricot notes is a great compliment to the pork as well as apples.

Nutritional Information (per serving).

Calories: 520; Protein: 50 g; Fat: 23 g; Sodium: 1024 mg; Cholesterol: 180 mg; Saturated Fat: 10 g; Dietary Fiber: 2 g; Carbohydrates: 21 g.

Apricot-Glazed Ham.

Yields: 20 servings.

Preparation time: 15 mins Cook time: approx. 2 hours.

Comments: A simple glaze over pork makes for a very easy unique celebration dish that is for a large event. Remember you can scale down the recipe. **Ingredients**.

5 pound fully prepared entire boneless pork 1/3 cup securely loaded brown sugar.

1tablespoon corn starch 1/2 tsp nutmeg 1/4 teaspoon cloves.

2/3 cup apricot nectar.

2tablespoons lemon juice.

Preparation and Cooking

1. Area pork on rack in a shallow roasting frying pan. Bake, exposed, in a 325 level F. stove for 1 1/4 hours or till meat thermostat signs up 140 degrees F. (concerning 15-18 minutes per extra pound.).

2. For the polish, in a small pan incorporate brownish sugar, cornstarch, nutmeg and also cloves. Stir in apricot nectar and also lemon juice. Cook over tool warmth up until thickened and bubbly, mixing continuously.

3. Brush ham with glaze. Continue baking 15-20 minutes much more, cleaning periodically with polish.

Suggested Wine: Pinot Grigio.

Nutritional Information (per serving).

Calories: 208; Protein: 25 g; Fat: 9 g; Sodium: 1572 mg; Cholesterol: 64 mg; Saturated Fat: 3 g; Dietary Fiber: 0 g; Carbohydrates: 6 g.

Baked Ham with Sweet 'n Sour Plum Sauce.

Yield: 24 servings.

Preparation time: 15 mins Cook time: 1 hour 15 minutes.

Remarks: Another vacation pork dish that will delight your family and friends. Great and also simple for your vacation party.

Ingredients.

6 extra pound fully-cooked boneless smoked ham.

1- 15-oz can purple plums packed in hefty syrup, drained pipes, pitted and mixed.

1cup crushed pineapple packed in juice, undrained.

1/4 cup eco-friendly onion, sliced.

1/4 mug brown sugar, firmly loaded.

2tablespoons seasoned rice a glass of wine vinegar 2 tbsps honey.

1 tbsp corn starch 1 tsp ginger, grated.

1 clove garlic, diced (1/2 tsp) 1/8 tsp Chinese five flavor.

Preparation and Cooking

1. Rating ham by making diagonal cuts in a ruby pattern. Area pork on rack in shallow toasting pan. Bake in preheated oven at 325 levels F. for 1 hour, 30 mins to 1 hr, 45 mins or until meat thermostat registers 140 degrees F.

2. At the same time combine staying **Ingredients** in tool saucepan. Serve boil; lower heat. Cook as well as mix for 2 minute longer. Remove from warmth.

3. Brush ham with sauce every 15 minutes throughout last half an hour of cooking.

4. Eliminate to serving plate as well as outdoor tents with aluminum foil. Allow stand 15 minutes. Brush with sauce. Carve and serve with remaining sauce.

5. If preferred, garnish with environment-friendly onion blossoms, wedges of fresh plums and unpeeled pineapple.

Recommended wine: Northern design Riesling which gets on the leaner side.

Nutritional Information (per serveing).

Calories: 202; Protein: 6 g; Fat: 6 g; Sodium: 1396 mg; Cholesterol: 60 mg.
; Saturated Fat: 2 g; Dietary Fiber: 0 g; Carbohydrates: 11 g.

Lovely Baked Lemon Sole.

Yield: 4 servings.

Preparation time: 15 mins Cook time: 21 minutes.

Remarks: This baked sole is excellent anytime however it does make an unique dish throughout the holiday season.

Ingredients.

4 (3-1/4 oz.) single fillets.

2 tsp fresh parsley, sliced 2 tsp margarine, melted.

1/8 tsp pepper.

2 tsp lemon juice 1/8 tsp paprika.

2 tbsp all-purpose flour.

Prep work as well as Cooking.

1. Rinse fillets thoroughly in cool water; pat completely dry with paper towels, as well as alloted.

2. Integrate thawed margarine as well as lemon juice in a little dish.

3. Incorporate flour, chopped parsley and pepper in a shallow container.

4. Dip fillets in margarine mixture and dredge in flour mixture. Transfer fillets to a nonstick flat pan, and sprinkle any type of staying margarine blend over fish.

5. Sprinkle fillets with paprika. When checked with a fork, Bake at 375 degrees F. for 15 to 20 minutes or up until fish is golden brown and also flakes quickly.

6. If a crisper appearance is desired, broil baked fillets 4 inches from warm for 1 minute. Garnish each fillet with a lemon wedge as well as fresh parsley sprigs, if preferred.

Suggested Wine: Sauvignon Blanc.

Nutritional Information (per serving).

Calories: 92; Protein: 16 g; Fat: 1 g; Sodium: 79 mg; Cholesterol: 50 mg; Carbohydrates: 3 g; Dietary Exchanges: 2 Lean Meat.

Baked Christmas Cornish Hens.

Yield: 4 Servings.

Prep: 70 min. Bake: 1 hour.

Comments: Make it easy on yourself-- cook Cornish hens with a simple basmati rice, dried apricot as well as almond stuffing all in one recipe. To save time, begin with precooked basmati rice, sold in pouches in the rice section.

Ingredients.

2 Cornish game hens (20 to 24 ounces each).

· 2-1/4 mugs reduced-sodium chicken brew.

· 2/3 cup raw wild rice 1/4 cup sliced onion.

1/4 mug cut celery 1 teaspoon olive oil.

1 garlic clove, diced.

1/2 cup cut dried out apricots 2 tablespoons chopped almonds 1 cup apricot nectar, divided.

1/2 mug pleasant gewurztraminer or apple juice, split 1/4 teaspoon plus 1/8 tsp salt, split.

1/4 tsp fowl spices 1/4 tsp pepper, separated.

1 teaspoon white balsamic vinegar Dash ground cinnamon.

Preparation and Cooking

1. In a small pan, bring broth and rice to a boil. Reduce warmth.

2. Simmer and cover for 60-70 mins or until rice hurts and also liquid is taken in.

3. In a nonstick frying pan, sauté onion and also celery in oil till tender. Add garlic; cook 1 min much longer.

4. Mix in the apricots, tsp salt, poultry flavoring and also 1/8 teaspoon pepper. Mix into prepared rice.

5. Spoon mix into 4 piles in a superficial roasting pan coated with food preparation spray; leading each with a Cornish chicken fifty percent.

6. Cover and also bake at 375 ° for 45 mins. Uncover; bake 15-20 mins longer or up until a thermometer reviews 180 °

7. In a big saucepan, incorporate staying nectar and red wine. Bring to a boil; cook for 5-7 mins or up until decreased to 1/2 mug.

8. Include the vinegar, cinnamon and also continuing to be salt and pepper.

Decrease heat; cook and also mix over medium-low warmth for 1 minute. Serve with hens and rice.
Recommended Sides: A green veggie as well as cranberry pleasure makes for a scrumptious and cheery meal.
Suggested Wine: Chablis.
Nutrition Information (per serving): 610 calories, 28 g fat (7 g saturated fat), 174 mg cholesterol, 744 mg sodium, 47 g carbohydrate, 4 g fiber, 37 g healthy protein.

Beef Tenderloin with Cranberry Balsamic Sauce.

Yield: 8 to 10 servings.

Preparation time: 20 mins Cook time: 1 1/2 hrs (including standing time)

Comments: You can never go wrong with a beef tenderloin roast, including the cranberry sauce provides it a precise vacation presentation.

Ingredients.

1 whole beef tenderloin roast (about 4 to 5 extra pounds) 2 tbsps cut fresh thyme.

1 tablespoon pepper.

1/3 mug balsamic vinegar.

3 tbsps carefully sliced shallots.

1 can (16 ounces) entire berry cranberry sauce 1/4 tsp salt.

Prep work as well as Cooking.

1.Pre-Heat stove to 425 ° F. 2. Combine thyme and pepper; get 1 tsp spices mix for sauce. Press continuing to be flavoring mix uniformly onto all surface areas of beef roast.

3. Area roast on shelf in superficial toasting pan. Place ovenproof meat thermostat so suggestion is focused in thickest component of beef. Do not add water or cover. Roast in 425 ° F stove 50 to 60 mins for tool uncommon; 60 to 70 minutes for medium doneness.

4. Remove roast when meat thermometer signs up 135 ° F for tool unusual; 150 ° F for tool. Transfer roast to carving board; outdoor tents loosely with aluminum foil. Allow stand 15 to 20 minutes. (Temperature will certainly remain to rise around 10 ° F to reach 145 ° F for medium uncommon; 160 ° F for tool.). 5. At the same time prepare sauce. Combine vinegar and shallots in small pan; serve a boil. Minimize warmth; simmer 3 minutes. Mix in cranberry sauce; bring to a boil. Decrease heat; simmer 6 mins to mix tastes, mixing periodically. Remove from heat; mix in reserved seasoning and also salt. 6. Carve roast into pieces; serve with sauce. Suggested a glass of wine: Nice Cabernet Sauvignon

Nutritional Information (per serveing).

Calories: 441; Protein: 5 g; Fat: 14 g; Sodium: 191 mg; Cholesterol: 134.mg; Saturated Fat: 5 g; Dietary Fiber: 1.1 g; Carbohydrates: 26 g.

Herbed Pepper Rubbed Boneless Pork Loin Roast.

Yield: 6-8 servings with leftovers.

Preparation time: 20 minutes Cook time: 1 hr as well as 10 minutes

Comments: Nice pork dish with a touch of spice. Easy to prepare

Ingredients.

1(3 pound) boneless pork loin roast Herbed Pepper Rub **Ingredients**:.
2tablespoons black pepper, broken.

2 tablespoons Parmesan cheese, grated 2 teaspoons dried out basil.

2 teaspoons dried out rosemary 2 tsps dried thyme 1/4 tsp garlic powder 1/4 teaspoon salt.

Preparation and Cooking

1. Rub pork dry with paper towel.

2. In tiny bowl, combine all rub **Ingredients** well and also relate to all surfaces of the pork roast.

3. Location roast in a shallow pan and also roast in a 350 levels F. stove for 1 hour (20 minutes per extra pound), till interior temperature on a thermostat checks out 145 levels F.

4. Eliminate roast from oven; allow remainder concerning 10 mins prior to cutting to serve.

Recommended a glass of wine: Red Burgundy.

Nutritional Information (per serveing).

Calories: 131; Protein: 22 g; Fat: 5 g; Sodium: 97 mg; Cholesterol: 57 mg; Saturated Fat: 1 g; Dietary Fiber: 1 g; Carbohydrates: 1 g.

Red Snapper on Ratatouille.

Yield: 4 servings.

Preparation time: 15 min Cook time: 40 min.

Comments: What an excellent way to serve Red Snapper, just tasty.

Ingredients.

4 (5-ounce) fillets red snapper, skin on 3 tbsps olive oil, divided.

1 large eggplant (regarding 1 pound), cut and trimmed into tiny dice (about 3 mugs).

1medium onion, reduced into little dice (concerning 1 1/2 cups) 2 cloves minced garlic (concerning 2 tsps).

2medium zucchini (1 extra pound overall), cut, cut right into little dice (about 2 1/2 mugs).

1 (14.5-ounce) can no-salt-added diced tomatoes.

1teaspoon herbs de Provence (or 1/2 tsp dried out thyme as well as 1/4 tsp each dried out rosemary as well as dried marjoram).

3/4 tsp salt, plus much more for flavoring 1/2 teaspoon freshly ground black pepper.

1/4 cup sliced fresh basil leaves, plus a lot more for garnish 2 teaspoons lemon juice.

2teaspoons rosemary (or other herb) infused olive oil, optional.

Prep work as well as Cooking.

1. In a big nonstick frying pan, warmth 1 tablespoon olive oil over medium-high warmth. Include the eggplant and also chef, stirring, till eggplant has softened however not entirely lost its shape, concerning 5 minutes. Remove the eggplant from frying pan.

2. Heat one more tablespoon of oil in the very same frying pan over medium-high warmth.

3. Include the onions and chef up until soft and also translucent, concerning 5 mins.

4. Include the garlic and zucchini to the frying pan as well as cook, stirring periodically, until the zucchini is soft, concerning 6 to 7 mins.

5. **Yield** eggplant to frying pan as well as add tomatoes, natural herbs de Provence, 1/2 teaspoon salt and 1/4 tsp pepper. Simmer roughly 10 minutes.

6. Season with added salt, to taste. Stir in basil and also eliminate from

warm.

7. To cook fish, preheat griddle.

8. Sprinkle fillets with 1/4 teaspoon salt and also 1/4 tsp pepper. Combine the remaining tablespoon olive oil with the lemon juice and brush on fillets.

9. Broil until fish is prepared and firm, regarding 7 mins.

10. Mound 1 mug ratatouille on 4 plates; leading each pile with 1 fish fillet and drizzle with 1/2 teaspoon natural herb instilled oil, if using. Garnish with extra basil.

Suggested sides: Tossed eggplant, zucchini and salad ratatouille.

Suggested wine: Chardonnay.

Nutritional Information (per serving).

Calories 314; Total Fat: 12.5 grams; Saturated Fat: 2 grams; Protein: 33 grams; Total carbohydrates: 18 grams; Sugar: 9 grams; Fiber: 5 grams; Cholesterol: 52 milligrams; Sodium: 553 milligrams.

Pork Roast Stuffed with Bourbon-Glazed Fruits and Nuts.

Yield: 8 servings.

Preparation time: 35 minutes Cook time: 55 minutes (consisting of 10 mins relaxing time).

Remarks: Roast pork is a vacation requirement in the majority of houses, this specific pork roast is superior as well as will become a favorite.

Ingredients.

2 extra pound boneless solitary loin pork roast 1 tbsp dried out thyme.

2/3 cup bourbon.

2/3 cup hen broth 1 tbsp molasses 1/4 mug light lotion 1/4 teaspoon salt

Stuffing **Ingredients**:.

1/2 mug matched days, coarsely chopped 1/4 cup dried out apricots, coarsely cut 1/4 cup pecans, carefully chopped.

1 clove garlic, crushed.

1-1/2 tsps dried thyme 1 tbsp molasses.

1/4 teaspoon salt.

1/4 tsp black pepper.

Prep work as well as Cooking.

1. Warm stove to 350 degrees F. In a medium dish, toss with each other all packing **Ingredients**, set aside.

2. In a large pan, incorporate bourbon, brew as well as molasses; give a boil, eliminate from warm and also alloted.

3. Butterfly (cut lengthwise mostly all the way through) the pork loin. Lay open and rub flat.

4. Beginning the center of the opened up loin, butterfly once more on the left side. Butterfly once more on the right-hand man side, lay open as well as pat flat. Equally spread out padding over loin.

5. Roll the loin up, like a jelly roll, and also link securely at 2-3 inch intervals with kitchen area twine; area in a shallow roasting pan, sprinkle with the.

tablespoon of thyme as well as pour bourbon mixture over.

6. Roast 40 minutes (regarding 20 mins per extra pound), basting occasionally with bourbon glaze, up until internal temperature on a

thermometer checks out 145 degrees F.

7. Get rid of roast from stove; let rest regarding 10 minutes.

8. Remove pork from pan, scheduling the drippings; keep warm. Add lotion and also 1/4 tsp salt to pan drippings. Prepare over medium-high heat, mixing regularly, till slightly enlarged. Cut pork, getting rid of twine as needed, and arrange on serving platter. Serve with frying pan sauce. Suggested wine: Red Zinfandel.

Nutritional Information (per serveing).

Calories: 262; Protein: 27 g; Fat: 9 g; Sodium: 190 mg; Cholesterol: 70 mg. ; Saturated Fat: 2 g; Carbohydrates: 17 g.

Cinnamon Apple Pork Tenderloin.

Yield: 4 servings.

Preparation time: 15 minutes Cook time: 1 hour.

Comments: You can never fail serving pork tenderloin during the holiday season(or any various other time for that matter). This is a simple yet delicious rendition.

Ingredients.

1lb pork tenderloin.

2apples, peeled, cored, sliced 2 tbsp cornstarch.

2 tbsp raisins.

1 tsp ground cinnamon.

Instructions.

1. Preheat the oven to 400 F.

2. Location the pork tenderloin in a toasting frying pan or casserole recipe with a cover.

3. Incorporate the staying **Ingredients** in a bowl and also mix. Spoon the apple mix around the pork tenderloin. Cover and cook 40 mins.

4. Get rid of the cover and spoon the apple combination over the tenderloin. **Yield** to the stove as well as cook 15-20 minutes longer up until tenderloin is browned and also prepared with.

Suggested a glass of wine: Gewürztraminer.

Nutritional Information (per serveing).

Calories: 270; Protein: 20 g; Fat: 10 g; Sodium: 148 mg; Carbohydrates: 13 g.

Exchanges: 3 Medium Fat Meat; 1 Fruit.

Sour and also wonderful Brisket.

Yield: 10 servings (size: 4-ounces brisket plus 3 tablespoons of sauce)

Preparation time: 20 minutes Cook Time: 3 humans resources. 10 min.

Comments: While this is a good vacation dish, it is a good dish anytime. This specific recipe is a great discussion.

Ingredients.

1 (3-pound) beef brisket, flat-half or first-cut cut, cut of any type of excess fat.

1 teaspoon salt.

1/2 teaspoon fresh ground black pepper 2 tbsps canola oil.

1 tool onion, reduced in 1/2, then very finely sliced right into 1/2 moons 3 cloves garlic, cut (concerning 1 tablespoon).

One 15- oz. can tomato sauce, preferably no salt added 1/4 mug low-sodium chicken brew or water.

3 tbsps securely loaded dark brown sugar 1/3 cup plus 1 tbsp cider vinegar.

1/3 cup raisins.

5 black peppercorns.

1 allspice berry.

Preparation and Cooking

1. Pre-heat the oven to 300 degrees F.

2. Rub the brisket dry and sprinkle with the salt and pepper.

3. Warm 1 tbsp of the oil over medium-high warmth in a Dutch stove or braising pot.

4. Scorch the brisket till it is browned, 4 to 5 minutes per side. Transfer the brisket to a plate.

5. Add the staying 1 tablespoon oil to the pot and cook the onion, stirring a few times, until softened, 3 to 5 minutes.

6. Include the garlic as well as cook, stirring, for 1 min.

7. Add the tomato sauce, broth, brown sugar, 1/3 mug of the vinegar, raisins, peppercorns, and also allspice as well as mix to integrate well.

8. Bring mixture to a boil, **Yield** brisket as well as any gathered juices to the pot, spoon several of the tomato-vinegar combination over the brisket, cover firmly, as well as transfer to the stove.

9. Prepare till the brisket is fork tender, 2 1/2 to 3 hrs.

10. Get rid of the brisket from the oven, move the meat to a cutting board, and let remainder for 10 to 20 minutes or, if serving later on, cover as well as refrigerate the meat and also sauce for numerous hrs or over night.

11. When you are ready to serve, cut the meat versus the grain right into 1/4-inch thick slices.

12. Stir the continuing to be 1 tbsp vinegar into the warm sauce.

13. **Yield** the chopped brisket to the sauce up until warmed with, after that serve.

Suggested a glass of wine: Cabernet Sauvignon.

Nutritional Information (per serveing).

Calories 360; Total Fat 12 grams; Saturated Fat 4 grams; Protein 46 grams; Total Carbohydrate 14 grams; Fiber 1 gram; Cholesterol 94 milligrams; Sodium 330 milligrams.

HANNUKAH RECIPES.

These meals are advised for Hanukah dinners however are delicious for any type of party or vacation.

Beef Rib Roast with Lemon Glazed Carrots and also Rutabagas.
Yield: 8 to 10 servings.

Preparation time: 20 minutes Cook time: Approx. 2 1/2 hours.

Comments: This is a have to have beef supper for the holidays. See if your regional butcher will trim the rib roast as well as eliminate the back bone, it will certainly save you a lot of time.

Ingredients.

1 well cut beef rib roast (2 to 4 ribs), tiny end, chine (back) bone removed (6 to 8 extra pounds).

Salt and also pepper.

4 to 5 medium carrots, cut right into 3 x 1/4 x 1/4 inch strips 1 small rutabaga, reduced into 3 x 1/4 x 1/4 inch strips.

1/2 cup water.

2 tbsps butter.

1 tbsp loaded brown sugar 1 tbsp fresh lemon juice 1/2 tsp grated lemon peel 1/4 tsp dried dill weed.

1/4 tsp salt.

Preparation and Cooking

1. Warm oven to 350F. Area roast, fat side up, in shallow roasting frying pan. Put ovenproof meat thermostat so suggestion is centered in thickest part of beef, not resting in fat or touching bone. Do not include water or cover.

2. Roast 2-1/4 to 2-1/2 hours for tool rare; 2-3/4 to 3 hrs for tool doneness.

3. When meat thermostat registers 135F for medium uncommon; 150F for tool, remove roast. Transfer roast to sculpting board; outdoor tents freely with light weight aluminum foil. Let stand 15 to 20 mins. (Temperature will remain to rise about 10F to get to 145F for medium uncommon; 160F for medium.).

4. At the same time, place carrots, rutabaga as well as water in medium pan. Cook as well as cover over medium heat 13 to 15 mins. Integrate butter, brownish sugar, lemon juice, lemon peel, dill weed and also 1/4 tsp salt in tiny frying pan; cook over medium warmth 2 to 3 minutes, mixing occasionally.

5. Include butter mix to veggies; continue food preparation, uncovered, 3 to 4 mins or up until veggies are polished, mixing periodically.

6. Sculpt roast into slices; season with salt as well as pepper, as desired. Serve with veggies.

Suggested Wine: Cabernet Sauvignon.

Nutritional Information (per serveing).

Calories: 364; Protein: 48 g; Fat: 15 g; Sodium: 199 mg; Cholesterol: 122 mg; Saturated Fat: 6 g; Dietary Fiber: 1.5 g; Carbohydrates: 7 g.

Lemon and Orange Roasted Turkey

Yield: 9 servings or lots of leftovers

Preparation time: 25 mins, plus 3 -8 hrs marinade time Cook time: 2 3/4 - 3 hrs, plus 15 -20 mins remainder time

Comments: Two words; Delicious and Festive

Ingredients

6-8 Pound entire turkey, washed and also drained 1/4 Cup frozen lemon juice concentrate defrosted 1/4 Cup fresh lemon juice

1/4 Cup honey 1/4 Cup olive oil

3 Tablespoons fresh lime juice

3 Tablespoons fresh chopped mint leaves 1 Tablespoon grated orange peel

2 Teaspoons grated lemon peel 1 Teaspoon grated lime peel off 1/3 Cup orange juice

Pinch salt and also pepper 1/4 Teaspoon cumin 1/4 Teaspoon cinnamon Pinch thyme

1red onion cut

Preparation as well as Cooking

1. Preheat oven to 325 degree F.

2. In a big dish, integrate all juices, honey, oil, mint, citrus peels, salt, pepper, herbs and also seasonings. Mix well. Add turkey to the combination, turning a few times to cover with sauce.

3. Top turkey with sliced onions.

4. Cover dish with aluminum foil. Marinade turkey in the fridge for 3-8 hrs.

5. When ready to roast, eliminate turkey from marinade as well as dispose of onions. Pour marinate into a saucepan as well as serve a boil, boil for 5 minutes. Reserve.

6. Location turkey, breast side up, on a rack in a large shallow (regarding 2-1/2 inches deep) roasting pan. Put oven-safe meat thermostat into the thickest part of the upper leg, bewaring the pointed end does not touch the bone.

7. Roast turkey in preheated stove about 2-3/4 to 3 hours. Baste turkey often with marinate as it chefs. If required, loosely cover with light-weight aluminum foil to prevent too much browning.

8. Continue to roast up until the thermostat registers 180 degrees F. in the upper leg, or 170 levels F. in the breast.

9. Get rid of turkey from the stove as well as permit it to relax for 15-20 minutes before carving.

Suggested red wine: Chardonnay or a Viognier which is a completely dry gewurztraminer with peach & apricot flavor.

Nutritional Information (per serveing).

Calories: 200; Protein: 26 g; Fat: 9 g; Sodium: 90 mg; Cholesterol: 75 mg; Carbohydrates: 2 g.

Traditional Corned Beef Brisket with Roasted Vegetables and Lemon-Mustard Sauce.

Yield: 4 servings.

Preparation time: 30 mins Cook time: 3 1/2 hours.

Ingredients.

3-1/2 to 4 extra pounds boneless corned beef brisket with flavoring packet 6 tool cloves garlic, peeled.

2teaspoons black peppercorns 2 mugs water.

1pound carrots, reduced right into 2-1/2 x 1/2-inch items 1 extra pound parsnips, cut right into 2-1/2 x 1/2-inch pieces 1 extra pound Savoy cabbage, cut right into 4 wedges.

2tablespoons olive oil 1/2 tsp salt.

1/4 tsp ground black pepper Lemon-Mustard Sauce (dish complies with).

Prep work as well as Cooking.

1. Placement oven racks in upper as well as lower thirds of oven. Heat oven to 350F.

2. Location corned beef brisket in roasting pan; spray garlic, **Ingredients** of seasoning packet and also peppercorns around brisket. Include water; cover securely with light weight aluminum foil. Braise in upper 3rd of 350F stove 3 to 3-1/2 hours or until brisket is fork-tender.

3. Meanwhile, location carrots, parsnips as well as cabbage on rimmed baking sheet. Drizzle with oil and toss delicately to layer. Period with salt and ground pepper. Cover with aluminum foil. Roast in lower 3rd of 350F oven with brisket 55 minutes. Reveal; proceed roasting 10 to 15 minutes or up until veggies are tender and begin to brownish.

4. Remove brisket from toasting pan. Cover and also cool 1/2 of brisket (regarding 12 ounces), 3/4 mug each parsnips and also carrots and also 1/2 mug Lemon-Mustard Sauce for Corned Beef and Roasted Vegetable Salad with Lemon-Dill Dressing.

5. Sculpt remaining brisket diagonally across the grain right into slim pieces. Serve with staying roasted vegetables and Lemon-Mustard Sauce.

6.Lemon-Mustard Sauce: Heat 1 tbsp olive oil in small saucepan.

over medium warm. Include 2 tbsps carefully sliced shallot; cook as well as mix regarding 2 mins or up until tender. Eliminate from warmth; cool 1 minute. Mix in 2/3 mug dairy products sour cream, 1/3 mug Dijon-style mustard, 1 tablespoon lemon juice, 1 tablespoon cut fresh dill as well as 1 teaspoon honey. Period with 1/4 tsp each salt as well as pepper. Cover; reserved.

Nutritional Information Per Serving.

Calories: 394; Protein: 20 g; Fat: 26 g; Sodium: 1682 mg;.

Cholesterol: 93 mg; Saturated Fat: 9 g; Dietary Fiber: 5.5 g; Carbohydrates: 23 g.

Lime Roast Chicken.

Yield: 6 servings.

Preparation time: 30 minutes, plus 1 hr to season. Prepare time: 1 hour

Comments: Moist as well as lush! Recipe can be doubled (or tripled) for firm. Reheats and/or ices up well.

Ingredients.

31/2 lb. (1.6 kg) entire poultry.

Salt & freshly ground pepper, to taste 1 tsp. dried basil.

3 limes.

1or 2 stalks celery, cut right into pieces.

1/4 c. cut parsley or coriander (cilantro).

Preparation and Cooking

1. Preheat stove to 425 levels F.

2. Rinse hen and also dry well. Loosen skin; rub seasonings inside the dental caries as well as under skin of chicken. Press juice of one lime over poultry.

3. Marinate for 1 hour at room temperature or cover and marinade in the refrigerator overnight.

4. Pierce limes with a fork. Location limes, celery and parsley inside the poultry. Close openings with steel skewers. Location hen on its side in a roasting pan.

5. Roast exposed for 20 mins. Turn poultry onto its opposite side and roast 20 minutes a lot more.

6. Reduce heat to 350 levels F and also roast breast side up 20 mins much longer, until crisp as well as golden.

7. Eliminate chicken from stove. Stress fat from pan juices. Location pan juices in a gravy watercraft. Cut up hen; remove skin, limes, celery and also parsley. Garnish with additional lime pieces.

Nutritional Information (per serveing).

Calories: 191; Protein: 28 g; Fat: 7.4 g; Sodium: 92 mg; Cholesterol: 84 mg.

; Carbohydrates: 1 g; Dietary Exchanges: 3-1/2 Low-Fat Meat.

LATKES.

Latkes are serveed at Chanukah to celebrate the miracle of a little bit of oil lasting for 8 days.

Cleo's Cabbage Latkes.

Yield: 10-12 servings Serving dimension: 1 latke **Preparation time**: 25 mins Cook time: 8 mins.

Remarks: When frying latkes, remember - with each brand-new batch, spray the pan with nonstick cooking spray and/or clean the frying pan with oil sometimes. You require to be client with latkes and also fry them for a long time until they are cooked through, or they will break down when flipped.

Ingredients.

2cups cabbage, finely grated 1 whole egg plus 2 egg whites 1 scallion, cut. 2 tablespoons soy or whole-wheat flour salt and pepper to preference. non-stick food preparation spray 1 tablespoon canola oil.

Preparation and Cooking

1. Place the cabbage in a 4-cup dish. With a wood spoon, mix in the eggs and scallion. Add flour and season to taste.

2. Utilizing damp hands, create latkes.

3. Fry on both sides over medium-high warm.

Nutritional Information (per serveing).

Calories: 46; Protein: 1.6 g; Fat: 2.5 g; Sodium: 28 mg; Cholesterol: 50 mg. ; Dietary Fiber: 1.5 g; Carbohydrates: 2.5 g Dietary Exchanges: 1 veggie; 1/2 Fat.

Broccoli Latkes.

Yield: 16 servings, serving dimension: 1 latke **Preparation time**: 15 minutes Cook time: 8 minutes.

Remarks: You can replace cauliflower or spinach for cauliflower to make a selection. Bear in mind frying pointer in the Cabbage Latkes dish.

Ingredients.

2 eggs plus 2 egg whites 1 small onion, peeled off.

1(2-pound) plan of frozen broccoli or 1 fresh head, steamed and drained pipes.

2tablespoons soy or whole-wheat flour salt and also pepper to taste.

non-stick cooking spray.

2 tbsps olive oil, for frying non-stick food preparation spray.

Preparation and Cooking

1. Let icy cauliflower thaw.

2. Place in colander as well as squeeze out the liquid.

3. Refine eggs as well as onion in food mill as well as include cauliflower, soy or routine flour and seasonings till finely chopped; do not over process.

4. Wipe a non-stick frying pan with a paper towel dipped in oil and spray the pan with non-stick cooking spray. Place on reduced heat, wait up until warm as well as decrease batter by tablespoonful right into pan. Brown on both sides.

Nutritional Information (per serveing).

Calories: 37; Protein: 2.8 g; Fat: 1.8 g; Sodium: 72 mg;; Dietary Fiber: 1 g. ; Carbohydrates: 2.5 g; Dietary Exchanges: 1 veggie; 1/2 Fat.

No-fry Potato and also Spinach Latkes.

Yield: 24 tool latkes or 6 lots minis. (3 minis equivalent 1 tool latke.).

Preparation time: 25 minutes Cook time: 20 mins.

Remarks: Traditional latkes are typically fried in 1/4 cup of oil, so 1 latke consists of concerning 3 grams of fat. I do not know anyone that can stop at simply 1 latke, so these "no-guilt" latkes are an excellent option. Each one consists of just over a gram of fat.

These latkes can be frozen for later on. Serving them with salsa, tzadziki, low-fat sour lotion or yogurt makes them extremely delicious.

Ingredients.

4 tsp. canola or vegetable oil, divided 3 medium Idaho potatoes.

10 oz. package frozen cut spinach, thawed and also pressed dry 1 medium onion.

1or 2 carrots.

2tbsp. diced fresh dill (or 2 tsp. dried out dill) 2 eggs plus 2 egg whites (or 3 eggs).

1/4 c. flour (whole or white wheat) 1/2 tsp. baking powder.

3/4 tsp. salt 1/4 tsp. pepper.

Preparation and Cooking

1. Area stove shelfs on the most affordable and center settings in your oven. Preheat oven to 450 degrees F.

2. Line 2 baking sheets with light weight aluminum foil. Spray with non-stick spray, after that clean each pan with 1 tsp. of oil. (This gives a crispy exterior to the latke.).

3. If you do not desire to peel them, Peel potatoes or scrub well. Utilizing the Grater of your processor, grate potatoes, making use of light pressure. Remove potatoes from processor.

4. Insert Steel Knife and also procedure spinach, onion, carrots and dill up until fine. Add grated potatoes, eggs, egg whites as well as staying 2 tsp. oil. Refine with fast on/offs to mix. Promptly assimilate staying **Ingredients**.

5. Drop combination by rounded does onto ready baking sheets. Squash slightly with the back of the spoon to form latkes.

6. Bake revealed at 450 levels F for 10 minutes, or till bases are nicely

browned and also crispy. Transform latkes over.

7. Transfer pan from the top shelf to the reduced shelf and also vice versa. Cook concerning 8 to 10 mins longer, or until brownish.

8. Serve instantly.

Nutritional Information (per serving).

Calories: 42; Protein: 2 g; Fat: 1.2 g; Sodium: 97 mg; Cholesterol: 18 mg; Carbohydrates: 6 g; Dietary Exchanges: 1/2 Bread/Starch.

Paul's Potato Latkes.

Yield: 10 latkes, 1 latke per serving.

Preparation time: 25 mins Cook time: 11 mins **Comments**: These potato latkes are outstanding! **Ingredients**.

2 mugs shredded and also peeled Russet potatoes, firmly stuffed (about 1 extra pound).

1/4 mug grated or finely chopped onion 1 big egg.

6 tbsps egg substitute.

2-3 tbsps reduced salt matzo meal (a little much less than 1 matzo, processed into fine crumbs).

1teaspoon salt.

2teaspoons canola oil.

Preparation and Cooking

1. Place the potatoes in a cheesecloth or dual density of paper towels and also wring to extract as much water out of the potatoes as feasible.

2. In tool bowl, stir the potatoes, onion, egg, egg alternative as well as matzo meal and also salt with each other well.

3. In a huge heavy-bottomed non stick skillet over medium-high heat, heat the oil until warm. Make sure the oil is spread equally over the bottom of the frying pan.

4. Location 1/4 mug (degree action) of potato mix right into the hot oil, pressing down on them to develop 1/4 to 1/2 inch thick patties. Spray tops with canola cooking spray. Brown on one side regarding 3 mins, pass on and brownish the opposite (about 3 minutes).

5. Serve these warm with applesauce, fat cost-free or light sour lotion and cut eco-friendly onions.

Nutritional Information (per serving).

Calories: 71; Protein: 3 g; Fat: 1 g; Sodium: 237 mg; Cholesterol: 21 mg; Dietary Fiber: 1 g; Carbohydrates: 12 g.

Zucchini Latkes.

Yield: 12 servings (serving size: 1 latke) **Preparation time**: 25 minutes
Cook time: 8 minutes **Comments**: Tastes excellent and also simple to do

Ingredients.

3large zucchini, peeled off 1 tool potato, peeled.

1egg plus 2 egg whites, beaten.

2tablespoons soy or whole-wheat flour salt and pepper to preference.

non-stick cooking spray 2 tablespoons canola oil.

Preparation and Cooking

1. Grate zucchini and also potato, either by hand or in a food mill. Drain
well in colander. Get rid of any kind of extra liquid by wrapping the grated
veggies in a tidy dish towel and also squeezing well.

2. By hand, mix in the egg, flour and also seasonings.

3. Oil a large non-stick frying pan.

4. Form latkes as well as location in frying pan.

5. Spray tops with cooking spray.

6. Fry on both sides, regarding 3 -4 minutes per side.

Nutritional Information (per serveing).

Calories: 40; Protein: 1.6 g; Fat: 2.2 g; Cholesterol: 27 mg; Dietary Fiber:.
0.5 g; Carbohydrates: 3.5 g; Dietary Exchanges: 1 vegetable; 1/2 Fat.

DESSERTS.

Christmas Cake.

Yield: 12 servings.

Preparation time: 25 minutes Cook time: 1 hour.

Comments: Soaking time for the fruit is not consisted of in the

Preparation time".

Ingredients.

11/2 mugs sultanas 1/2 mug raisins.

2tablespoons brandy.

1 tablespoon water.

1 cup sieved pumpkin puree (no swellings) 2 eggs, beaten.

1/2 mug apple juice concentrate.

1/2 cup skim milk or 1/2 mug low-fat milk 1/2 cup cut pecans.

1 teaspoon ground cinnamon 1 teaspoon combined flavor.

1 cup self-rising flour.

1 mug entire dish self-rising flour 1/2 teaspoon bicarbonate of soft drink

Preparation and Cooking

1. Mix the sultanas, raisins, brandy as well as water, and after that saturate overnight.

2. Mix sieved pumpkin, eggs, apple concentrate and milk.

3. Include the soaked fruit, nuts and also flavors, after that filtered flour and bicarbonate of soda. **Yield** bran left in sieve to powder blend. Mix well with wood spoon.

4. Spoon right into a gently oiled 20cm cake tin.

5. Bake for 10 minutes at 200C, then deny the heat and bake at 180C till prepared via as well as browned. (approx. 1-1/4 hrs).

6. Making use of the apple concentrate provides the sweet taste to this cake.

Nourishment Information (per serveing).

Calories: 194.0; Calories from Fat: 39; Total Fat: 4.3 g; Saturated Fat: 0.6 g; Cholesterol: 31.2 mg; Sugars: 20.7 g; Sodium: 208.8 mg; Total Carbohydrate: 35.7 g; Dietary Fiber: 1.9 g; Protein: 3.9 g.

Old Fashion Christmas Pudding.

Yield: 10 Servings.

Preparation time: 30 mins Cook time: 5 hours.

Remarks: This no-sugar Christmas dessert will be appreciated by everybody; the apples as well as carrots maintain it wet and also the cinnamon and mixed spice warm it well-- definitely a delightful desert.

Ingredients.

1. 1/2 mug ordinary flour.

2. 1/2 cup fresh white breadcrumbs.

3. 1/2 cup shredded veggie suet.

4. 1/2 mug currants.

5. 3/4 cup raisins.

6.1 tbsp low-calorie sugar.

7.2 tsp each ground cinnamon and also mixed flavor.

8.1 1/2 tsp cooking powder.

9.4 huge eggs, defeated.

10. Finely grated passion of 1 large lemon.

11. Finely grated passion of 1 big orange.

12.2 carrots, cut and finely grated.

13.2 dessert apples, peeled off, cored as well as reduced into tiny chunks.

14. 3/4 cup milk.

15. Icing sugar, for dusting.

Preparation and Cooking

1. Gently butter a 2-quart baking dish as well as line the base with a circle of baking paper.

2. Mix with each other the dry **Ingredients**, then stir in the other **Ingredients** till well combined. Spoon the mixture into the basin and also cover with a circle of buttered cooking paper. Fold a pleat right into a piece of aluminum foil and arrange over the dessert. Protect with string.

3. Thoroughly position the dessert in a frying pan of boiling water, ensuring the water comes a third of the method up the side of the basin.

4. Cover, lower the warmth to a simmer as well as steam gently for 5 hrs.

5. Turn out the dessert as well as serve cleaned with topping sugar. Nutritional details (per serving).

Calories: 331k; Fat: 14.9 g; Saturated fat: 6.8 g; 7.2 g Protein 7.2 g; Carbs: 45.4.g; 24.9 g Sugar: 24.9 g; Salt: 0.6 g.

Apple Pie.

Yield: 8 servings.

Preparation time: 25 mins Cook time: 40 minutes.

Comments: What would Christmas be without a delicious homemade apple pie? This is a good one.

Ingredients.

Bread for 2 crust 9" pie.

6-7 big apples, peeled off, cored, cut.

1/2 cup fruit sweetener (1/4 cup frozen apple juice concentrate plus 1/4 mug granulated fructose).

2 tsp cinnamon.

1 tsp nutmeg.

1 tablespoon margarine.

Preparation and Cooking

1. Pre warmth oven to 350 levels F.

2. Line pie bottom with bread.

3. In huge bowl, incorporate **Ingredients** except margarine. Mix well and spoon into pastry lined frying pan. Populate with margarine.

4. Cover with leading crust, seal, and also flute edges. Cut a few little slits in crust. Cook 40 minutes, or till crust is gold brown.

Nutritional Information (per serving).

Calories: 298; Protein: 3 g; Fat: 14 g; Sodium: 140 mg; Cholesterol: 0 mg; Carbohydrates: 42 g; Dietary Exchanges: 2 Bread, 1 Fruit, 2 Fat.

Wendy's Christmas Pudding.

Yield: 4 servings.

Preparation time: 20 minutes Cook time: 1-- 2 hrs, plus saved in fridge for one week. After that reheated for 45 mins.

Remarks: I recommend that after it has been prepared, shop it in the refrigerator so the tastes can grow.

* Don't forget to make a wish when you mix the Christmas Pudding!

Ingredients.

4 tablespoons of sultanas 3 tablespoons of raisins 2 tbsp of currants.

1/3 cup grated carrot, apple or cooked pumpkin (or combination of 2) 3 tbsps of brandy.

1 tsp of ground cinnamon 1/2 teaspoon of nutmeg.

1 & 1/2 pieces of whole meal bread, crumbed 1/3 cup of skim or reduced fat milk.

1 tablespoon brown sugar or sweetener 1 tbsp of hot water.

skin of an orange, grated.

1 & 1/2 mugs of whole dish flour 1 teaspoon combined spice.

2tablespoons of margarine 1 egg lightly beaten.

1 tsp vanilla significance.

1/2 tsp bicarbonate of soda 2 teaspoons of Parisian significance

Preparation and Cooking

1. Soak dried fruit, orange peel, carrot, apple or pumpkin in brandy overnight.

2. Add bread crumbs.

3. Add egg, milk, fruit blend, vanilla, Parisian essence and also sugar or sweetener.

4. Mix bicarb soft drink and warm water well with various other

Ingredients.

5. Put right into a greased dish, cover securely and heavy steam for 1 - 2 hours.

6. Store in the fridge for one week.

7. Reheat by steaming, boiling 30- 45 minutes till heated up through or microwave for about 6-7 minutes.

8. When prepared, turn out and also serve with brandy sauce.

Nutritional Information (per serving).
Calories: 298; Cholesterol: 46g; Protein: 10g; Fat: 6gm.

***Blueberry Crumb Cake.**

Yield: 9 to 12 Servings.

Preparation time: 25 minutes Cook time: 40 mins.

Remarks: In the holiday spirit this crumb cake is most proper and also I almost attempt you to eat simply one piece.

Ingredients.

4 tbsps margarine.

1 egg.

5-1/2 tsps "Equal for Recipes" or 18 packages Equal sweetener 1 mug all-purpose flour.

1-1/2 tsps baking powder 1/2 tsp cooking soft drink.

1/4 tsp salt.

1 tsp ground cinnamon 1/2 cup reduced-fat buttermilk 1/2 teaspoon vanilla. Blueberry Crumb Topping (dish adheres to) Blueberry Crumb Topping

Ingredients.

1/3 cup all-purpose flour.

3-1/2 tsps Equal for Recipes or 12 packages Equal sugar 1 tsp ground cinnamon.

1/2 teaspoon maple remove.

4 tbsps chilly margarine, cut into items 1 cup fresh, or iced up, blueberries. Prep work as well as Cooking.

1. Pre-heat the oven to 350 levels F.

2. Beat margarine, egg, and also Equal for Recipes in tool dish till smooth. Mix in integrate flour, baking powder, cooking soda, salt, and also cinnamon alternately with consolidated buttermilk as well as vanilla, finishing as well as starting with dry **Ingredients**.

3. Put batter into greased and also floured 8-inch square cake pan; spray Blueberry Crumb Topping equally over batter.

4. Bake up until toothpick placed in cakes appears tidy, 35 to 40 mins. Serve warm.

5. Blueberry Crumb Topping Directions: Combine flour, Equal for recipes, and also cinnamon in little dish; sprinkle with maple essence. Cut in margarine up until combination looks like rugged crumbs. Toss as well as add blueberries.

Nutritional Information Per Serving.

Calories: 196; Protein: 6 g; Fat: 11 g; Sodium: 358 mg; Cholesterol: 24 mg;
Carbohydrates: 18 g.

Exchanges: 1 Bread/Starch, 2-1/2 Fat.

Keith's Cappuccino Pie.

Yield: 8 servings.

Preparation time: 30 minutesCook time: 5 mins Chill time: 3 Hours

Comments: I really do not recognize that this is a real vacation pie
however it sure tastes great.

Ingredients.

1/2 cup space temperature coffee.

1 envelope (1/4 ounce) unflavored gelatin 1/4 mug coffee liqueur.

1cup light or nonfat ricotta cheese Sugar replacement equivalent to 1/3 cup
sugar 1/8 teaspoon ground cinnamon.

2cups nonfat or light whipped topping 1 Chocolate Almond pie crust.

1-1/2 tbsps cut dark delicious chocolate.

Preparation and Cooking

1. Location 2 tablespoons of the coffee in a blender or food processor.
Sprinkle the gelatin over the coffee as well as allow sit for 2 mins.

2. Bring the remaining coffee to a boil as well as put over the combination
in the blender. Blend for 1 minute, till the gelatin is completely liquified.
Allot for 5 mins to cool down slightly.

3. Add the liqueur to the mixer blend as well as mix to blend. Include the
ricotta, sugar substitute, as well as cinnamon and mix till smooth. Put the
mixture right into a big dish and cool for about 30 mins, or until the
consistency of dessert. Whisk up until smooth and afterwards fold in the
whipped topping.

4. Spread out the ricotta mix into the piecrust, swirling the top.

5. Spray the chocolate over the top.

6. Cover as well as chill for at least 3 hrs, or up until set.

Nutritional Information Per Serving.

Calories: 208; Protein: 7.2 g; Fat: 7 g; Sodium: 128 mg; Cholesterol: 1 mg;
Dietary Fiber: 1.1 g; Carbohydrates: 27 g; Dietary Exchanges: 2

Carbohydrate: 1-1/2 Fat.

Mother's Carrot Cake.

Yield: 12 servings.

Preparation time: 30 mins Cook time: 1 1/4 hrs plus 10 mins cooling

Comments: One of my favorite whenever, not just during the holidays.

Ingredients.

1-1/4 mugs whole wheat flour Pinch of salt.

2-1/2 tsps cooking powder 1 tsp ground cinnamon.

1 tsp ground ginger 1/2 mug light brown sugar.

3/4 cup raisins, drenched over night in 1/2 cup unsweetened orange juice 4 medium carrots, peeled off and also carefully grated.

1tablespoon sunflower oil.

2medium egg whites, at area temperature level.

3-1/2 ounces low-fat lotion cheese defeated with 2 teaspoons looked confectioners' sugar.

Preparation and Cooking

1. Preheat the stove to 325 levels F.

2. Lightly oil an 8 x 4 inch loaf pan and line it with parchment paper.

3. Look the flour, salt, cooking powder, cinnamon and ginger into a large bowl, tipping in any kind of bran left in the sifter.

4. Mix in the sugar, raisins with their juice, carrots as well as oil as well as mix well.

5. Beat the egg whites till they stand up in soft optimals, after that fold gently however completely right into the carrot mix, making use of a big spoon or spatula.

6. Pour into the frying pan and cook in the center of the stove for regarding 1-1/4 hrs, or until a skewer placed in the facility appears clean.

7. Cool in the frying pan for 10 minutes, after that end up onto a cake rack and also remove the lining paper. When totally awesome, halved flat and full of the sweetened lotion cheese.

Nutritional Information (per serving).

Calories: 137; Protein: 4 g; Fat: 3 g; Sodium: 154 mg; Cholesterol: 5 mg; Saturated Fat: 1 g; Dietary Fiber: 3 g; Carbohydrates: 26g; Dietary Exchanges: 1 Starch, 2/3 Fruit, 1/2 Fat.

HOLIDAY COOKIES.

Typical Thumbprint Cookies.

Yield: 15 cookies.

Preparation time: 4 mins Cook Time: 15 mins.

Comments: Fun to do as well as delicious too.

Ingredients.

· 1/2 mug butter or 1/2 mug margarine, softened.

· 1 egg.

· 1/2 teaspoon vanilla.

· 1/4 -1 3/8 mugs flour.

· 1/2 mug sliced nuts.

· tsps sweetening agent.

· tbsps diabetic person sugar-free jam or 2 tbsps sugar-free jelly.

Preparation and Cooking

1. Beat with each other butter, egg, vanilla, as well as adequate flour so dough is no longer sticky.

2. Work in nuts.

3. Chill until firm sufficient to roll and also shape into spheres.

4. Position on ungreased cookie sheet.

5. Dip thumb in flour.

6. Press strongly in middle of each cookie.

7. Cook 15 mins or until golden brown on the bottom (350F).

8. Get rid of from stove.

9. Sprinkle with sweetening agent.

10. Enable to cool down.

11. Fill hollows with jam or jelly.

12. Maintain cooled.

Hermit Cookies

Yield: 48 cookies
Preparation time: 20 minutes Cook time: 15 minutes
Comments: Another tasty traditional Christmas cookie
Ingredients
  ½ cup shortening
  ½ cup brown sugar substitute
  2 eggs
  2 cups all-purpose flour
  1 tsp. Baking powder
  1 tsp. Cinnamon
  ¼ tsp. Salt
  ¼ tsp. Baking soda
  ¼ tsp. Nutmeg
  ¼ tsp. Clove ground
  1/3 cup 1% milk
  1 cup raisins
  ¾ cup walnuts chopped
Preparation and Cooking
  1. Preheat oven at 350
  2. Grease cookie sheets.
  3. Cream together shortening and brown sugar substitute. Add eggs, until light and fluffy.
  4. Combine flour, baking powder, cinnamon, salt, baking soda, nutmeg and cloves to the shortening mixture; mix well.
  5. Fold in raisins and Walnuts.
  6. Drop by teaspoons onto lightly greased baking sheets about 2 – 3 inches apart.
  7. Bake in the upper third oven shelf at 350 for 12 – 15 minutes or until lightly brown.
Nutrition Information (per serving)
Calories: 89; Fat: 7g; Cholesterol: 10mg; Sodium: 60mg; Carbohydrate: 14%

Peanut Butter Cookies

Yield: 48 cookies
Preparation time: 20 minutes Total Time: 29 minutes
Comments: Peanut butter cookies are a favorite. Easy recipe.
Ingredients
1/4 cup margarine, softened
1 cup creamy style peanut butter
1/4 cup egg substitute
2 tablespoons honey
1/2 teaspoon vanilla extract
1 cup Splenda sugar substitute (or any powdered sugar substitute that is the equivalent of 1 cup of sugar)
1 1/2 cups all-purpose flour
1/2 teaspoon baking soda
1/2 teaspoon
Directions
1. Preheat oven to 350° F.
2. In a large bowl, beat margarine and peanut butter with an electric mixer until creamy, approximately 1 minute.
3. Add egg substitute, honey and vanilla.
4. Beat on high speed for approximately 1½ minutes.
5. Add Splenda and beat on medium speed until well blended, approximately 30 seconds.
6. In small bowl, combine flour, baking soda and salt.
7. Slowly add flour mixture to peanut butter mixture, beating on low speed until well blended, about 1½ minutes (mixture may be crumbly).
8. Roll level teaspoons of dough into balls and drop onto a lined sheet pan, about 2" apart.
9. Flatten each ball with a fork, pressing a crisscross pattern into each cookie.
10. Bake 7-9 minutes or until light brown around the edges.
11. Cool on wire rack.

Nutrition Information (per serving – 2 cookies)
Calories: 116.3; Calories from Fat: 67 ; 57%; Total Fat: 7.4g 11% ; Saturated Fat: 1.4g 7% ; Cholesterol: 0.0mg 0% ; Sodium: 151.0mg 6% ; Total

Carbohydrate: 9.5g 3% ; Dietary Fiber: 0.8g 3%; Sugars: 2.4 g 9% ; Protein: 3.8g 7%

Raspberry Fig Linzer Cookies

Yield: 26 servings
Preparation time: 30 minutes Total Time: 35 minutes
Comments: Lot to the preparation, but easy. It is worth the effort
Ingredients
Dough
2 tablespoons sweet butter, softened
1/4 cup Splenda sugar substitute, for baking
1/2 teaspoon baking powder
2 tablespoons vegetable oil (canola is best)
1/8 teaspoon salt
1 eggs or 1/4 cup egg substitute
1/2 teaspoon vanilla
2 cups sifted cake flour (measure after sifting)
3 tablespoons cornmeal (either yellow or white)
Filling
1/3 cup orange juice
1/3 cup fresh raspberries or 1/3 cup frozen raspberries
3 tablespoons dried figs, finely diced
Assembly
powdered sugar
cake flour
Preparation and Cooking
1. In a large bowl beat together the butter, oil, sugar substitute until combined. Add in the egg/egg substitute, salt, baking powder and vanilla.
2. Using your mixer, beat in the corn meal and as much of the flour as you can. If the dough becomes too stiff, mix in the rest of the flour by hand.
3. Divide the dough in half, wrap in plastic and chill for two hours.
4. While the dough is chilling, prepare your filling by adding all **Ingredients** to a small saucepan.
5. Bring the mix to a boil and reduce to a lower simmer. Cook for 5 minutes, stirring regularly, until the filling is thickened.
6. Transfer to a mini-chopper or use an immersion blender to puree the mix until smooth. Allow to cool completely.

7. Preheat oven to 375 degrees. (Note you are using untreated cookie sheets here.)
8. Roll out the first disc of dough until it is 1/8 inch thick. Using the larger cookie cutter, cut out cookies and transfer to the baking sheet about 1 inch apart.
9. Bake for 5 minutes until the edges of the cookie are firm but not browned. Remove from oven and transfer to a wire rack.
10. With the second disc of dough, repeat as above except that you will be using the smaller cutter to create a window in the cookies for the tops. In doing so, carefully place the smaller cookie cutters on the shapes made by the larger cutters in a manner so that the sides around the center hole are even.
11. To assemble the linzer cookies, first apply a light dusting of powdered sugar on the top cookies (those with the cutouts). Spread a small amount of the raspberry-fig filling on the bottom cookie. Gently take the top cookies by the edges and line the top cookie over the filling pressing down ever so slightly.

Nutrition Information (per serving)

Calories: 66.3; Calories from Fat: 20 30%; Total Fat: 2.2g; Saturated Fat: 0.7g;

Cholesterol: 10.4mg: Sugars: 0.9 g; Sodium: 21.6mg; Total Carbohydrate: 10.1g;

Dietary Fiber: 0.4g; Sugars: 0.9 g; Protein: 1.2g

Christmas Fruitcake Cookies

Yield: 3 dozen cookies
Preparation time: 20 minutes Cook time: 10 minutes
Comments: Easy to do and taste like a fruitcake, real Christmassy
Ingredients:
- 1/2 cup Vegetable oil
- 1/2 cup Brown sugar
- 1 Egg
- 1 1/4 cup Whole wheat flour
- 1/2 tsp Baking powder
- 1 tsp Ground cinnamon
- 1/4 tsp Ground cloves
- 1/4 tsp Ground allspice
- 1/4 cup Milk
- 1/2 cup Chopped walnuts
- 1/2 cup Raisins
- 1/2 cup Snipped dried apricots
- 1/2 cup Chopped dates

Preparation and Cooking
1. Pre heat oven to 350 degrees F
2. Cream together the oil and sugar.
3. Add the egg. Then blend in the remaining **Ingredients**.
4. Drop by spoonfuls onto a lightly oiled baking sheet.
5. Bake in oven for about 10 minutes. Cool on a wire rack and store in a tightly closed container.

Nutritional Information (per serving, 1 cookie) - 77 calories, 1/2 fruit exchange, 1 fat exchange 9 grams carbohydrate, 1 gram protein, 4 grams fat 7 mg sodium, 70 mg potassium, 8 mg cholesterol

Molly's Molasses Ginger Cookies

Yield: 4 dozen
Preparation time: 1 hour 10 minutes (includes chilling time) Cook time: 25 minutes
Comments: Cook in several batches, will be chewy and good.
Ingredients
- nonstick cooking spray
- 1/3 cup margarine, softened (not spread or tub product)
- 1/3 cup Splenda brown sugar blend, packed
- 1 teaspoon baking soda
- 1 teaspoon ground ginger (or to taste)
- 3/4 teaspoon ground cinnamon (or to taste)
- 1/4 cup Egg Beaters egg substitute
- 1/4 cup dark molasses
- 1 1/2 cups all-purpose flour
- 1/2 cup whole wheat flour
- 1/4 cup Splenda granular
- 1 teaspoon ground cinnamon

Preparation and Cooking
1. Preheat oven to 35 degrees F.
2. Spray cookie sheet with nonstick spray; set aside.
3. In a large mixing bowl, beat the margarine with an electric mixer on medium to high speed for 30 seconds.
4. Add the brown sugar, baking soda, ginger, and 1/2 teaspoon cinnamon; beat until combined.
5. Beat in Eggbeaters and molasses.
6. Beat in as much of the all-purpose and whole wheat flour as you can with the mixer.
7. Stir in any remaining flour with a wooden spoon.
8. Cover and chill in the refrigerator for 1 hour.
9. Shape dough into 1-inch balls.
10. Combine the granulated Splenda and 1 teaspoon cinnamon.
11. Roll balls in Splenda-cinnamon mixture.
12. Place 2 inches apart on prepared cookie sheet.
13. Bake in oven for 10 to 11 minutes or until set and tops are cracked.
14. Remove from cookie sheet.

15. Cool on a wire rack.

16. Makes about 4 dozen.

Nutrition Information (per serving)

Calories: 34.0; Calories: from Fat 11; Total Fat: 1.3g; Saturated Fat: 0.2g;
Cholesterol: 0.0mg; Sodium: 42.0mg; Total Carbohydrate: 5.0g;
Dietary Fiber: 0.3g; Sugars: 0.0 g; Protein: 0.6g; 1%

Peppermint Chocolate Cookies

Yield: 3 dozen cookies
Preparation time: 15 minutes – plus overnight in refrigerator. Cook time:
10 -12 minutes per batch
Comments: Cookies will be soft if kept in an airtight container. If you want
them crisp, freeze them or keep them in a container that is not airtight.
Ingredients
- 1 cup margarine(2 sticks)
- 1 1/3 cup Sugar
- 1 tsp peppermint, flavoring
- 1/2 cup egg whites at room temperature
- 3 cups All-purpose flour
- 1/2 cup cocoa
- 2 tsp baking powder
- 1/4 tsp Salt

Preparation and Cooking
1. Pre heat oven to 350 degrees F.
2. Cream margarine and sugar together at medium speed until light and
fluffy.
3. Add flavorings and egg whites, and mix at medium speed for 1 minute,
scraping down bowl before and after adding flavorings and egg whites.
4. Stir flour, cocoa, baking powder and salt together to blend well; add to
creamy mixture.
5. Mix at medium speed to blend well.
6. Cover and refrigerate from 3 hours to overnight.
7. **Yield** dough to room temperature. Roll our on a lightly floured board
to 1/4 thick. Cut with a 2 1/2 round cutter or an equivalent cutter.
8. Place on cookie sheets that have been sprayed with pan spray or lined
with aluminum foil. Bake in oven for 10 to 12 minutes, or until cookies
are almost firm.
8. Remove cookies to a wire rack and cool to room temperature.
Nutritional Information (per serving)
Calories: 115, FAT: 5g, CHO: 16g, Na: 98mg, PRO: 2g, Cholesterol: 0;
Dietary Exchanges: 1 Starch/bread exchange + 1 Fat exchange

Marvelous Macaroon Cookies

Yield: 42 cookies
Preparation time: 15 minutes Cook time: 20 minutes
Comments: A marvelous cookie that can be mixed up in a jiffy!
Ingredients
    1-1/2 cups flaked coconut
    1/2 cup sugar
    1/4 cup flour
    1/4 tsp salt
    3 egg whites at room temperature
    1/2 tsp vanilla extract
    1/2 tsp almond extract
Preparation and Cooking
1. Preheat oven to 325°F. Line 2 baking sheets with parchment paper or aluminum foil.
2. In medium bowl, use a rubber spatula or wooden spoon to combine coconut, sugar, flour and salt. Stir in egg whites and extracts until well blended. Drop by rounded teaspoonful on prepared baking sheets.
3. Bake for 18-20 minutes, or until golden brown. Remove cookies on parchment paper or foil to rack to cool. When cool, remove from paper or foil and store in container.
Nutritional Information (per serving)
 Cal: 93; Total Fat: 9 g; Carb: 11 g; Cholesterol 00 mg; Sodium 57 mg; Fiber: 1 g; Sugars: 7 g; Dietary Exchanges: 1 Fruit; 1 Fat.

No Bake Christmas Cookies

Yield: 24-36 Cookies
Preparation time: 30 minutes Cook time: 1 hour
Comments: Easy to prepare and surprisingly good
Ingredients
6 tablespoons Nestle Quick Sugar-free Instant Chocolate Milk Mix
1 teaspoon vanilla extract
1/2 cup margarine
1/2 cup milk (I use 1%)
1 cup flaked coconut
3 cups quick oatmeal
Preparation
1. In food processor or mixer bowl add sugar, vanilla, margarine, milk and blend until smooth.
2. Add coconut and oatmeal and blend until mixed together well.
3. On a cookie sheet place a piece of wax paper and take spoonful of the mixture and roll into a ball place close together.
4. Ready to eat in 1 hour.
5. Keep in the refrigerator.

Nutrition Information (per serving)
Calories: 91.0; Calories from Fat: 50; Total Fat: 5.6g; Saturated Fat: 1.7g; Cholesterol: 0.7mg; Sugars: 1.5 g; Sodium: 55.1mg; Total Carbohydrate: 8.5g;
Dietary Fiber: 1.1g; Protein: 1.9g

Carrot Cake Cookies

Yield: 36 cookies
Preparation time: 30 minutes Cook time: 12 minutes per batch
Comments: For brown sugar substitute choose from Sweet'nLow® Brown,
or Sugar Twin® Granulated Brown. Follow package directions to use product
amount equivalent to 1/4 cup packed brown sugar.

Ingredients

- 1/2 cup honey
- 1/4 cup brown sugar substitute equivalent to 1/4 cup brown sugar
- 1 tablespoon unsalted butter, softened
- 1/4 cup canola oil
- 1 egg
- 1 egg white
- 3 cups shredded carrots (6 medium)
- 2 cups all-purpose flour
- 1/2 cup whole wheat flour
- 1 1/2 teaspoons pumpkin pie spice
- 1/2 teaspoon baking powder
- 1/2 teaspoon baking soda
- 3/4 cup chopped walnuts or pecans
- 2 ounces reduced-fat cream cheese, softened
- 1/2 cup powdered sugar
- 2 -3 teaspoons fat-free milk
- 1/4 cup chopped walnuts or pecans (optional)

Directions

1. Preheat oven to 350 degrees F.
2. Coat two large cookie sheets with nonstick cooking spray or line with parchment paper; set aside.
3. In a large bowl, combine honey, brown sugar, and butter; beat with an electric mixer on medium speed until well mixed.
4. Beat in oil, egg, and egg white. Stir in carrots.
5. In a medium bowl, stir together flours, pumpkin pie spice, baking powder, baking soda, and 1/4 teaspoon salt.
6. Add flour mixture to carrot mixture, half at a time, stirring until moistened after each addition. Stir in the 3/4 cup nuts.

7. Using a tablespoon measuring spoon, drop 36 mounds of dough 2 inches apart onto prepared cookie sheets. If desired, press with moistened fingers to flatten each mound slightly.
8. Bake for 10 to 12 minutes or until lightly browned. Transfer to wire racks; cool completely.
9. For drizzle, in a small bowl, combine cream cheese and powdered sugar; beat with an electric mixer on medium speed until well mixed. Beat in enough of the milk to make a drizzling consistency.
10. Drizzle over cooled cookies. If desired, sprinkle with the 1/4 cup nuts.

Nutrition Facts (per serving)

Calories: 189; Potassium: 131 mg; sodium: 109 mg; Monosaturated fat: 3 mg; Polyunsaturated fat: 3g; Fiber: 2 g; Sugar: 15 g; Carb: 27g; Fat, total: 8 g; Chol.: 16 mg; Sat. Fat: 1 g; Trans fatty acid: 0g; Pyridoxine: 0 mg; Niacin: 1mg; Riboflavin: 0 mg; Thiamin: 0; mg Protein: 4 g; Iron: 1 mg; Calcium: 30 mg; Calcium: 200 kcal; Folate: 36 µg; Diabetic Exchanges: Carb Choice 2; Fat: 1.5; Starch: 1

CONCLUSION

The holiday diabetes recipes presented in this cookbook are not just ordinary but rather quite special. This is only one of the diabetes cookbooks in a collection of Dick's Diabetes Cookbooks available on Amazon's Kindle.

If you are fortunate enough to have purchased any of these cookbooks then you now have a collection of terrific diabetes recipes including side dishes and salads. The, soon to be released, diabetes desserts cookbook will give you a full library of delicious diabetes cookbooks.

The important thing to remember is that just because you are a diabetic, or you are cooking for a family member or friend with diabetes, it does not mean that your meals have to be bland and dull. Diabetic cooking, done properly, is tasty, healthy, and meets the requirements of a diabetic lifestyle.

I know you will enjoy preparing these holiday season meals that I have personally selected. Your family and friends are really going to be impressed with your new found cooking skills.

I look forward to serving your needs as a diabetic home cook in my future diabetes cookbooks. If you have a question or suggestion, feel free to send me an email at: dicksdiabetescookbook@gmail.com .

Here's to Good, Healthy Cooking and Enjoyable Eating - this and every holiday season!

DIABETIC EXCHANGE LIST

The exchange lists are for diet and meal planning. The lists are food groups that are similar in dietetic content. Each list has foods that have approximately the same amount of carbohydrate, protein, fat and calories. In the amounts given, all choices on each list are equal. Any food on the list can be exchanged or traded for any other food on the list. The lists are grouped into three main groups: carbohydrate group; meat and meat substitute group; and fat group.

The carbohydrate group contains the starch, fruit, milk, other carbohydrates and vegetable lists. Grouping foods this way allows for more convenient exchange among these lists and more flexibility in choosing foods. The meat and meat substitute group contains very lean, lean, medium-fat, and high-fat meat and substitute lists. The fat group contains monounsaturated, polyunsaturated and saturated fat lists

The following Food Exchange List is from information provided by the American Dietetic Association.

Use these food exchange lists to check out serving sizes for each group of foods and to see what other food choices are available for each group of foods.

Vegetables
Fat-Free and Very Low-Fat Milk
Very Lean Protein
Fruits
Lean Protein
Medium-Fat Proteins
Starches
Fats

Vegetables contain 25 calories and 5 grams of carbohydrate. One serving equals:

½ C Cooked vegetables (carrots, broccoli, zucchini, cabbage, etc.)

1 C Raw vegetables or salad greens

½ C Vegetable juice

If you're hungry, eat more fresh or steamed vegetables.

Fat-Free and Very Low-Fat Milk contain 90 calories per serving. One serving equals:

1 C Milk, fat-free or 1% fat

¾ C Yogurt, plain nonfat or low-fat

1 C Yogurt, artificially sweetened

Very Lean Protein choices have 35 calories and 1 gram of fat per serving. One serving equals:

1 oz. Turkey breast or chicken breast, skin removed
1 oz. Fish fillet (flounder, sole, scrod, cod, etc.)
1 oz. Canned tuna in water
1 oz. Shellfish (clams, lobster, scallop, shrimp)
¾ C Cottage cheese, nonfat or low-fat
2 Egg whites
¼ C Egg substitute
1 oz. Fat-free cheese
½ C Beans, cooked (black beans, kidney, chick peas or lentils): count as 1 starch/bread and 1 very lean protein

Fruits contain 15 grams of carbohydrate and 60 calories. One serving equals:

1 small Apple, banana, orange, nectarine
1 med. Fresh peach
1 Kiwi
½ Grapefruit
½ Mango
1 C Fresh berries (strawberries, raspberries, or blueberries)
1 C Fresh melon cubes
1/8th Honeydew melon
4 oz.
 Unsweetened juice
4 tsp. Jelly or jam

Lean Protein choices have 55 calories and 2–3 grams of fat per serving. One serving equals:

1 oz. Chicken—dark meat, skin removed
1 oz. Turkey—dark meat, skin removed
1 oz. Salmon, swordfish, herring
1 oz. Lean beef (flank steak, London broil, tenderloin, roast beef)*
1 oz. Veal, roast or lean chop*
1 oz. Lamb, roast or lean chop*
1 oz. Pork, tenderloin or fresh ham*
1 oz. Low-fat cheese (with 3 g or less of fat per ounce)
1 oz. Low-fat luncheon meats (with 3 g or less of fat per ounce)
¼ C 4.5% cottage cheese

2 med. Sardines

* Limit to 1–2 times per week

Medium-Fat Proteins have 75 calories and 5 grams of fat per serving. One serving equals:

1 oz. Beef (any prime cut), corned beef, ground beef**

1 oz. Pork chop

1 Whole egg (medium)**

1 oz. Mozzarella cheese

¼ C Ricotta cheese

4 oz. Tofu (note this is a heart healthy choice)

** Choose these very infrequently

Starches contain 15 grams of carbohydrate and 80 calories per serving. One serving equals:

1 slice Bread (white, pumpernickel, whole wheat, rye)

2 slices Reduced-calorie or "lite" bread

¼ (1 oz.) Bagel (varies)

½ English muffin

½ Hamburger bun

¾ C Cold cereal

1/3 C Rice, brown or white, cooked

1/3 C Barley or couscous, cooked

1/3 C Legumes (dried beans, peas or lentils), cooked

½ C Pasta, cooked

½ C Bulgar, cooked

½ C Corn, sweet potato, or green peas

3 oz. Baked sweet or white potato

¾ oz. Pretzels

3 C Popcorn, hot air popped or microwave (80% light)

Fats contain 45 calories and 5 grams of fat per serving. One serving equals:

1 tsp. Oil (vegetable, corn, canola, olive, etc.)

1 tsp. Butter

1 tsp. Stick margarine

1 tsp. Mayonnaise

1 Tbsp. Reduced-fat margarine or mayonnaise

1 Tbsp. Salad dressing

1 Tbsp. Cream cheese

2 Tbsp. Lite cream cheese

1/8th Avocado
8 large Black olives
10 large Stuffed green olives
1 slice Bacon

REPORT - DIABETES and ALCOHOL

Beyond all the health and safety concerns about alcohol, if you have diabetes and are on diabetes medications that lower blood glucose, you need to practice caution. The action of insulin and some diabetes pills, sulfonylureas and meglitinides (Prandin), is to lower blood glucose by making more insulin. So, you should not drink when your blood glucose is low or when your stomach is empty.

Alcohol can cause hypoglycemia shortly after drinking and for 24 hours after drinking. So, if you want to drink alcohol, check your blood glucose before you drink and eat either before or while you drink. You should also check your blood glucose before you go to bed to make sure it is at a safe level – between 100 and 140 mg/dL. If your blood glucose is low, eat something to raise it.

The symptoms of too much alcohol and hypoglycemia can be similar – sleepiness, dizziness, and disorientation. You do not want anyone to confuse hypoglycemia for drunkenness, because they might not give you the proper assistance and treatment. The best way to get the help you need if you are hypoglycemic is to always wear an I.D. that states "I have diabetes."

Another problem with alcohol can be that it may lessen your resolve to stay on track with healthy eating. Contemplate this situation. You sit at a restaurant and sip a glass of wine while you peruse the menu. As you slowly relax your taste buds might be more easily tempted to overindulge.

A Few Guidelines

- If you choose to drink alcohol, limit the amount and have it with food. Talk with your health care team about whether alcohol is safe for you.
- Women should drink 1 or fewer alcoholic beverages a day (1 alcoholic drink equals a 12 oz. beer, 5 oz. glass of wine, or 1 ½ oz. distilled spirits (vodka, whiskey, gin, etc.).
- Men should drink 2 or fewer alcoholic drinks a day.
- If you drink alcohol at least several times a week, make sure your doctor knows this before he/she prescribes a diabetes pill.

More Tips to Sip By

- Drink only when and if blood glucose is under control. Do not omit food from your regular meal plan.
- Test blood glucose to help you decide if you should drink.
- Wear an I.D. that notes you have diabetes.
- Sip a drink slowly to make it last.

- Have a no calorie beverage by your side to quench your thirst.
- Try wine spritzers to decrease the amount of wine in the drink.
- Use calorie-free drink mixers: diet soda, club soda, diet tonic water, or water.
- Drink alcohol with a snack or meal. Some good snack ideas are pretzels, popcorn, crackers, fat-free or baked chips, raw vegetables and a low-fat yogurt dip.
- Find a registered dietitian to help you fit alcohol into your food plan.
- Do not drive or plan to drive for several hours after you drink alcohol.

Adapted from the book *Diabetes Meal Planning Made Easy, 4th Edition*, written by Hope S. Warshaw, MMSc, RD, CDE, a nationally recognized expert on healthy eating and diabetes.

Alcohol and diabetes: Drinking safely

By Mayo Clinic staff and Mayo Clinic diabetes educators, Nancy Klobassa Davidson, R.N., and Peggy Moreland, R.N.

Patients often ask whether they can drink alcohol. Most people with diabetes are aware of how different foods affect their blood glucose, but aren't sure if alcohol and diabetes is safe. The American Diabetes Association recommends that you ask yourself three basic questions:

- Is your diabetes under control?
- Check with your healthcare provider. Do you have health problems that alcohol can make worse, such as diabetic nerve damage or high blood pressure?
- Do you know how alcohol can affect you and your diabetes?

Alcohol and your body

When you drink an alcoholic beverage, the alcohol moves quickly into the bloodstream without being metabolized in your stomach. Within five minutes of having a drink, there's enough alcohol in your bloodstream to measure. Alcohol is metabolized by the liver, and for the average person it takes approximately two hours to metabolize one drink. If you drink alcohol faster than your body metabolizes it, the excess alcohol moves through your bloodstream to other parts of your body, particularly your brain. If you've ever gotten a "buzz" when drinking alcohol, that's why.

If you're on insulin, or certain oral diabetes medications, such as a sulfonylurea (glipizide, glyburide) or meglitinide (Prandin) that stimulate the pancreas to produce more insulin, drinking alcohol can cause a dangerous low blood sugar because your liver has to work to remove the alcohol from your blood instead of its main job to regulate your blood sugar.

Safe drinking guidelines

- Consult your physician and follow his/her advice — alcohol can worsen diabetes complications.
- Monitor your blood sugar before, during, and after drinking alcohol. Remember to check before going to bed.
- Never drink alcohol on an empty stomach — food slows down the absorption of alcohol into the blood stream.
- Avoid binge drinking — The American Diabetes Association suggests men have no more than two drinks a day, and women one, the same guidelines as for those without diabetes.
- Be prepared — Always carry along glucose tablets or another source of sugar. Glucagon shots will not work in this case.
- Don't mix alcohol and exercise — physical activity and alcohol will increase your chances of getting a low blood sugar.

The symptoms of too much alcohol and low blood sugar can be very similar, i.e. sleepiness, dizziness, and disorientation. You don't want others to mistakenly confuse hypoglycemia for drunkenness. Alcohol and diabetes is another reminder that it's always a good idea to wear a diabetes medical I.D.